Collected Works

Jacqueline Feldman

Ellicott Press
Washington, D.C.

Published by Ellicott Press, Washington, D.C.

Book design by Ray Rhamey

ISBN: 978-0-615-68556-4

Library of Congress Control Number: 2012947517

Table of Contents

I. Mothers

II. Children

III. Separation

IV. Endings

V. Perspectives

VI. A Singular Saga

To those who knew and loved Jackie Feldman,

and those who come after.

I. Mothers

A Lavender Box Revisited

I open the lid and faces
gaze, voices speak,
moments long-forgotten
materialize.

From among a potpourri
of siblings and cousins,
suddenly my children,
unblurred,
at three, six, eleven,
thirteen, and seventeen—
their poems, letters, and
New Year's resolutions
with wishes, hopes,
x's and o's,
vowing to do better,
tend pets, be satisfied,
patient, respectful,
spend wisely, be kinder
to brother, to sister . . .

Years have passed since they
scrambled to pack their bags,
carelessly leaving behind them
bits of themselves;
they are still here,
in this lavender box.
I had only to open the lid
to find them again.

Delivery (1856)

She lay pale and listless
against the pillows
until the midwife
brought the baby.
Then she turned away.
"No," she said. "This one
I cannot nurse."

Too often she had resurrected
from three tiny graves,
the others,
felt each breathing
at her breast again,
then wrenched from her arms
within a day.
Eighth month babies did not live.

Perhaps she'd been remiss
those times,
committed a sin unwittingly,
mixed two dishes, meat with milk,
or carried a kerchief
on the Sabbath.

But this time
she'd been vigilant,
working each task
with a critical eye,
repeatedly ripping out
some ritual until it conformed
to the strictest design.

Her lips unbidden
muttered prayers
on her way to market,
as her needles flew,
or watching from her doorway
the women nursing babies,
their easy laughter ringing
as they gossiped in the courtyard.

She'd shrugged away
the random claws of pain
that clutched her
midway through
the dreaded month,
but soon was prey
to spasm after spasm,
each barbed with its augury.

The doctor sent for now
to treat her minor lacerations
soon took his leave, yet lingered
to study her guarded face—
her eyes held by the farthest
rose that climbed the wall ahead—
then hastily set down his bag
and asked to see the child.

His practiced eye
surveyed that tiny form
sucking wildly on its fist.

"Frau Eisler," he said suddenly,
"you must have been mistaken.

This cannot be an eighth-month baby—
her finger nails have not yet grown.
But have no fear, Frau Eisler.
She is strong—and fortunately
still is in the *seventh* month."

His words reverberated
through the quiet room,
and when she felt the baby
in her arms,
echoed and reechoed
like a sounding
of the shofar
among the hills.

She lived to know
her children's children.

Her days ran out
before my own began,
leaving to the others
the echo of her words,
her syllables of song.

But from her portrait
on my wall, her oval face,
with high-piled hair
spilling to one shoulder,
gazes at me as I pass.

I look at that face and say,
"Grandma."

In the Labor Room

(Before Lamaze)

The pains were coming faster now,
turning my head from side to side
on the pillow. In second intervals,
I glimpsed my husband's pale face,
my mother's smile twisted
into a caricature of itself
at the foot of the bed.

In the next room, a woman
began to scream—a wild,
high-decibel, prolonged
scream—released unabashed
from deep within.

The sound held me enthralled,
drew me toward it and into it,
until I was inside it,
locked away from pain.

As it faded, I could feel its echo
in my throat, my voice returning
from some far-off place,
and as light mended
the fragmented faces before me,
a hand's gentle pressure on my own:
I was the woman who had screamed.

Then came the counterpoint—
the answering notes
of our baby's first cry.

Well-remembered Hands

waving, blowing
kisses, until you
turned the corner
on the way to school
each morning

floured, wrist-deep
in dough, releasing
aromatic clouds of
cinnamon
and sugar into
the warm kitchen

awakening arpeggios
of bass through treble
to chase invisible
motes of dust from
piano keys . . .

forever uprooting,
transplanting chairs
and tables, grafting
new groupings of
pictures on the wall,
somehow nudging the
baby grand to a newly uncovered oasis
(so that our father,
returning in the evening,
feared he'd set foot in
the wrong house) . . .

intuitively smudging
gold picture frames with
just the right amount
of white to impart
a gently-fused patina . . .

carefully thumbing
pages of Webster's or
Britannica to
dissolve heated
dinner-table
debates . . .

trembling, trying
to steady a thermometer
that could indisputably
proclaim a possible
prognosis . . .

arranging stray
blankets around you
in the bedroom's cold
darkness at 3 a.m. . . .

Two Deer

Half hidden, silhouetted
in the thicket
at the side of the road,
they stood facing each other,
transfixed by the discord
of my car's engine
in that peaceful neighborhood.

Not a crackle of twig,
not a rustle of leaf.
Yet I saw the huge brown
oval eyes of the older
speaking to the other
of memory, of danger,
of warning in a language
as eloquent as a human
tongue might have uttered.

Moments later, after
the car had stopped,
there they were,
sauntering down
the middle of the road
single file, mother and daughter
in lock step, tales swishing
in perfect time from side to side,
a rhythmic duet
in a world we had thought
was ours alone.

The Dressing

(To Natalie)

Defying every curve,
convexity, concavity,
she smooths the diaper
swiftly into place
averting chance
catastrophe—
effects with but
the merest scuffle
successful passage
of the head through
a most unlikely opening—
while within her grasp
tiny fists
resisting every tug
emerge from sleeves
with thumbs intact—
and last
two squirming legs
are guided firmly
to their footed
destination.

Beyond a doubt
in former days,
a little girl
whose gold-red curls
fringed raptest
concentration
learned to dress
her doll in sure
anticipation
of the woman
that would be.

II. Children

Below The Surface

(to Harold)

I remember how you held me,
a child of two, to let
my brother take your place
in the furious
teenage game nearby.

Some fool tripped you
as you stood knee-deep
in surf, and your shout,
a bolt of anger, throbbed
through my small body,
your hard arms
tightening about me.

A rippling rampart
rose above, crashed
around us as we fell.

Smooth translucency
consumed us, choked out
air and sound and sun,
scent of seaweed stung
my nostrils, briny
liquid gagged my tongue,
unceasing seas
surged over me.

Until we washed heaving
on the beach,
you never let me go.

Fractions

Fractions frightened her.
They leered at her with
skeleton teeth, grimaced
through Miss Morley's
crayoned crosses
that desecrated her neat
arithmetic papers.

Miss Morley had crossed
her out from day one
when she seated her midway
between the chosen ones
up front who ran errands
at her bidding and hardly
a safe distance from
William and the hulking
boys in back who had been
in fourth grade for years,
and were kept after school
almost every day.

Spitballs whizzed past,
paper clips twanged,
sometimes stung.
A sudden tweak of her hair.
A constant shuffling
and whispering from
their corner. One
day, a ragged note
from William asking
to borrow an eraser.

She looked back and
saw his praying hands,
pleading look.

Who she was had finally
caught up with her:
she was not who she
had been in third grade,
not who her teacher there
had told her she was,
not who everyone
thought she was.
Now she knew who she was.
Miss Morley had let
her know.

She bargained with God,
promising to be kind
to everyone from now on,
even her enemies, if He
would just let her learn
fractions so she could
sit up front with the
chosen ones.

I . . . DROP . . . COOKIE

The refrain, like the insistent
cries of a wounded animal,
swelled through the supermarket
above the hungry din
of last-minute shoppers.

I . . . DROP . . . COOKIE

No weeping, just three words
asking nothing of anyone,
interwoven with choked pauses
to defeat forbidden tears
poised to rush between them.

Again and again it sounded
from the depths of a grocery cart
where your large pale face
peered out of piles of produce:
I . . . DROP . . . COOKIE

She who wheeled you,
the merest hint of a smile
curling her thin lips, spoke
at last. "Well," she offered,
"it's on the floor now."

As I stood at the checkout
counter, your words still
resounded from the rear
of the store:
I . . . DROP . . . COOKIE

Even now, I hear your
little boy's voice
already old for your age,
already old enough to know that
nothing would be done about it.

The Chair

They used it as a ship
on rainy days,
its blue mohair depths
(made to fit their father's
long lean body) affording
room enough for two
plus cargo—toy hammers
for repairs, curly-haired doll,
small teddy bear, and
often forks and spoons,
though very little food,
perhaps because they fished
along the way.

They sailed for hours,
sometimes dropping anchor
at ports of call in
India, Australia, or Africa,
but never missing Red China,
from where, without changing
course, they made directly for
White China.

There they conversed with
the natives, whose language
they understood and spoke fluently.
Others, struggling to untangle
its linguistic knots,
could say only that phonetically
it faintly resembled
the Finno-Ugric tongue
their grandmother
sometimes used.

When we moved to the new house,
it was left behind—
a blue mohair chair in which
someone might settle back
to read the evening papers
without ever recognizing
its full potential—
how seaworthy
it really was.

Delayed Departure

A flock of birds flies out
from a flat rooftop.
It's time to head south.

But no. It arcs back
to the rooftop, and after
moments, circles around
again, repeating the ritual
over and over, day after day.

Can these be nestlings
of last summer,
now grown and eager
to be on the way,
yet not quite ready
for their first excursion?

And is a squad leader
coaching them up there—
some old bird, veteran
of untold odysseys—
observing practice runs,
regrouping them each time
to strengthen their defenses
against predators and storms,
drawing diagrams in the sandy
rooftop to illustrate
just where they erred?

One day
they will get it right,
fly off the rooftop, head
only south, recede
into the light that hovers
between fall and winter, carrying
with swift wings
the last crumbs
of summer.

To Jane

Your voice
undreamlike
comes to me in corridors
of crowded shopping malls
and ancient luncheon haunts,
in theatres in the beehive hum
before the curtain-call,
and all those mother-daughter places
we no longer share
these days.

Its customary tone
denies the differences
that separate us now—
contracting miles
of air and track as well—
and argues for your presence
in the nearby throng
somewhere.

Of course
you are not there.
But, as senselessly
I stop and stare,
I see you on a far-off street
snarled with hissing brakes
and bursting horns
and shouts and curses,
and I wonder if you hear me call
above the Babel'd air.

III. Separation

Decree Nisi

Only four
before the heavy door—
two next of kin
two counselors
case in hand—
fossil phrases
jokes exhumed
to exorcise embodiment
of what awaits within.

Door ajar
they're ushered in—
graved faces
muffled tread.

The obsequies begin—
ghosts scurry around,
closet skeletons grin,
specters from the past
slip in: a guileless bride,
unwary groom
watch intently
in the hollow room.

Rites performed,
peroration said,
the two bereaved
their lives undone
leave
one
by
one.

The Joust

We took up the matter.
Mightily.
Accusations clashed,
innuendoes rang
on ancient shields.
Steel barbs stung.

Cuts went deep,
spilling obloquy.
And when at last
you faltered,
I saw that
victory was mine.

Unabashed, I reveled
in your shame . . .

until your smile
a sudden wicked flash,
took aim,
touched quick,
pierced home.

Illusion

Once I strove to make you fit
the image that
with careless ease
I daubed across my mind
in reveries,
blocking you out
in boldest tints and hues,
infusing all your grays
with brilliant blues.

Since then I've learned
to mix your colors
straight from life,
apply my strokes
with utmost care—
no ambiguous glaze,
no artful themes—
and now I see before me
the uselessness of dreams.

Deception

Some lies you've told me have been sharp,
their shining knives
piercing through transparent parts.

And some were whispered in the dark
between permissive sheets
quickening my pulse's beats.

Some, half-clothed in robes of truth
you proffered me with pious pride,
believing them yourself.

And some you murmured into others' ears—
our private jests,
our secret jargon.

Then one day when hope had gone
and signs arrived that you could not deny
in trembling tones you spoke the truth at last.

It was a lie.

Final Encounter

We must have quickened pace
and somehow we are there—
at that last stronghold
where ruined walls
of books
rise up
between us.

Long ago
we'd closed
their ranks,
aligning them
in tight
proximity.

Now they are a barricade
over which we divide them,
yielding them
to each other
with careful fairness
and guarded looks.

Elegy

We pass each other,
you and I, as though
the rigid pattern
of a dance of long ago,
ghostlike, slow,
required us to pass
gracefully
without a glance.

And yet, to former strains
so close we've stepped
my breasts conspired
with your touch,
your thighs pressed mine.

We cannot hear
that music now
or find the rhythm
of the words we said,

and without a gasp or struggle,
without dying,
we are dead.

Reunion

You entered with studious care,
your greeting was lifelessly spare,
missing my lips
you kissed
the insensitive air.

By dinner glib comments had staled,
thought processes stubbornly failed,
eschewing sage concepts
our view
of the wontons prevailed.

The play could not tender a spark—
our hands never touched in the dark,
reaching to close that highly-charged
breach
they fell shy of their mark.

The wide waste of evening crossed,
over tea we absorbed the cost . . .
facing the way that we'd tried
to retrace
we found ourselves lost.

IV. Endings

Rezoning

Bare bones of building
rise
across the narrow way.
Day by day
teams of men and cranes
displace empty space
with limbs and joints
of steel.

Embedded deeply
in once-daisied earth,
its naked frame
will soon be fleshed
with brick or stone.

And after that,
in future years
who will know
that once there'd been
an evening view
when lights
would start to weave
through dusking walls,
while cars' approaching rays
sprayed the distant arc
of street
and charcoal branches,
seared by sky,
slowly smoldered
down to dark?

Summer Solstice

Now
earlier and earlier
the sun's impassive face
will slip
below the trees
slowly eroding
the unfolding days.

Now
secretly
this apogee of green
will start to wane,
nests lose their fervor,
crickets signal decadence,
humid breezes shoo
a few illicit leaves
across the grass.

Now
as we gather armfuls of summer
we fly on a course
toward winter and night,
unswervingly,
as from birth's moment
we begin
to die.

Flight's End

I found it heaped large
on my balcony floor,
the broken neck
tucked neatly under
grey feathers.

Inside, I came upon
the likeness
death had limned
high on my window.

The image on the glass
has long since washed away.
Its replica I hold within—
the smashed beak and
stunned eyes,
the defeated wings,
and in that darkening
before closure,
the insult
of incompletion.

The Cost

Plucked lately from its leafy height—
last August's gift to fallow fall—
one perfect peach, too dearly priced,
still beckons from the huckster's stall.

Shall I plumb its velvet depths
that wait beneath its sueded hue,
quaff its cache of silken liquor,
then die of thirst all winter through?

Autumn Dissidents

Some leaves linger,
            reluctant to fall,

stubbornly clinging
            to branches that birthed them,

daring to scorn
            earth's cyclical call.

Frayed with age, frail
            phantoms of their former days,

they still sport traces
            of last season's green

renewed by autumn rain.
            Now December,

provoking only palsied tremors,
            prods in vain.

Remembering summer,
            they remain.

The Hour

When the second stroke
left him powerless
between hospital sheets,
I was the one who could go
for the hour his nurse
would be delayed—
I, the youngest, a teen-
age girl, awed by this uncle,
a man of sixty-three who
corresponded with kings . . .

I straightened pillows,
tendered sips of water
through a straw.
It was later, when he
asked for the urinal,
that I faltered,
scanning the empty room
for someone—anyone—
who could tell me
it was all right . . .

My hand would only
slide the vessel
under the covers
so far—
not quite far enough.

Seconds passed . . . then
a violent agitation
of the bedclothes
as he taught his limp body
to counter my inadequacy.

His nurse appeared at the door;
I turned to leave.

He called to me.

"Please, before you go," he said,
"my . . . left shoulder is itching.
Would you rub it for me?"

Spare Parts

I've kept them on my shelf
for years, in a bulging
cardboard box.

There I'd always find
a new switch for my reading lamp,
an extra handle for the pan that
sautés mushrooms to a turn,
an emergency cord to revive
a failing percolator, and other
life-sustaining wires, screws,
and tiny bulbs ready
to minister to urgent
needs of aging objects.

Often years would pass before
I'd need some new spare part;
still, as soon as one was used,
I sought another, forged
from the same mold, so that
most today are clones
of clones, rare strains
for which I've traveled far.

But no longer do I rush to find
replacements, for now the mist
that used to hide what lies
ahead begins to clear, and
from here, I can discern a time
when percolator, lamp, and
frying pan will stand unheeded
and spare parts will stay
within their cardboard box
until they crumble and corrode.

V. Perspectives

Perspective from a 747

Blue lake mirage below
Locarno's graphite tip—
from here

a mere cross-country ski
upon a sweep
of clouds

snow-deep, untried—
a silent glide
unfettered, free

above me an indulgent sky
and on all sides
infinity.

Duplicity

Small bug crawls on glass
table: through window furtive
jet skims western sun.

The Showing

She greets you in the same
outmoded blouse-and-skirt
while her fine new frocks
hang fruitless
in the dark terrain
of dusty closets.

After tea, she displays
them: unabashed, she lifts
each plastic cover to expose
their virgin charms, holding
them, one by one, on high
for you to validate
in clearest light
their unstained fabric,
the unadulterated brilliance
of their hue.

Now and then, she realigns
a shoulder on its hanger,
smooths an imperceptible
crease, or adjusts a ruffle
gone astray, and with a final
loving pat, returns each
to its special place.

When at last she closes
the closet door,
its quiet click
remains with you,
so that even later,
after you have left her,
you hear it echo
down the corridor.

At the Market

Others crowd around
pears, apples, grapes—
and even oranges—
but not these oranges.

Here, we two
are alone
in a moment
mutely shared.

Faces grave, our eyes
look down upon
our common quest.
Yet secretly each smiles
in tribute to
the other's expertise.

Strangers, of course.
But in this one thing—
in our understanding
of these oranges—
we know each other well.

It is a communion
we carry with us
as we go
our separate ways

Harvey

In the late afternoon, when he'd
spread peat on the beds and
watered them, he would pause
to survey our tiny garden
as perhaps Wordsworth
might have paused to contemplate
his whole field of daffodils.
"Refreshing, isn't it?" he would say
if you told him how pleased you were.

Before leaving, he did not fail
to look back from the gate
to call, "See you Wednesday."

You would stand
at the door then
taking in his easy stride
as you mused upon the life
he hastened toward and
that certain Wednesday
that would lead him back
to you.

Watching him stride
up the street, I thought
of the sparkling currents
of his life that propelled
him swiftly onward now—
and the inconstant Wednesday
when they must ebb
back again to our doorstep.

Pinter Play

three on stage
two of one gender
triangle abstrusely
chatting bemusedly
of earlier days

remembrances clash
prior alliances hashed
and rehashed
old sequences change
into strange new
arrangements

emotions tripped
by innocent trivia
impasse awaits
the tilt of a glass—
the flick of an ash
can arouse the basest
of traits

civilized law proscribes
tooth and claw
but words can be used
with intent to kill
and when all has been said
victims fall
just as dead

exchanges on stage
charging the surface
cross-currents flow
short circuits below
an ampered allusion
magnetic pause . . .
and at the conclusion
high-voltage applause.

A True Story

The three have taken up residence
in my den.

I am timid about being left alone
with them, in awe of their superior
intelligence, the way they stare
at me, daring me to use them:

The computer with its mocking voice,
the fax machine's dogged mind-set,
the printer's noisy complaints
in words that might make me blush,
if I could translate them.

Although they are securely grounded,
their attitude implies habitation
in a higher sphere, far too
complex and sophisticated
for someone like me to reach.

Since their arrival, I have felt obliged
to do my writing at the kitchen table.
That is where I am sitting the other day,
when I hear a loud "Ping!" followed,
at regular intervals, by more loud pings.

When, breathless, I reach the den,
I notice that the fax machine
is in trouble. Despite being out of paper,
it struggles to receive a message.
But only low groans accompany its labors.

I glance at the computer; it merely
glares at me in disgust. Oddly,
it is the printer that is pinging.
However, all I can do for now
is feed the fax machine.

Instantly, the printer stops pinging,
and the message comes through:
my distributor wants a thousand
copies of my book ASAP.

I pause to consider the fax machine's
unflinching devotion to its task,
the computer's anger that now seems
justified, and the small printer
that never stopped pinging
until help arrived.

The late afternoon sun,
emerging from behind a cloud,
gilds the dull gray surfaces
of the three machines.
Their brilliance blinds me,
and I must turn away.

When I look again, all three
are smiling at me.

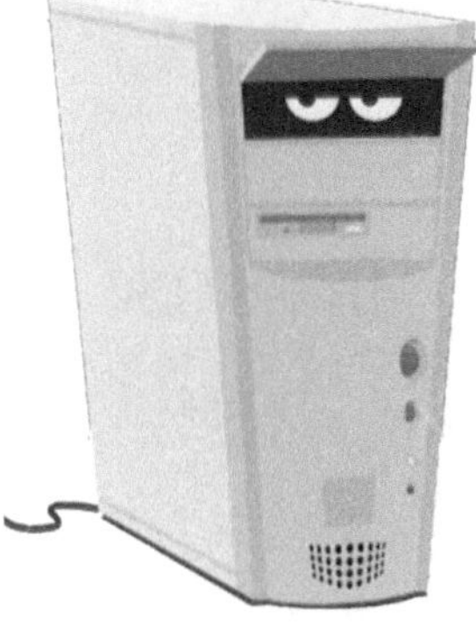

Free Verse

(to Paul)

Strange—
cowed by Stevens, Rilke,
Eliot, you've not seen fit
to write a poem; yet
last night
unwittingly
you left one
on my answering machine.

Surely it escaped
unnoticed
from a lyric cache
you keep confined
in some half-forgotten
closet of your mind.

If ever you unlocked
that door, who knows
to what vast heights
the rest might soar
to shine like stars
through space and time?

But this one,
addressed to me,
is mine.

Thesis

Terminated reading . . .
books in stacks of four
placed for easy reaching . . .
it all adds up so neatly
aesthetically speaking . . .
how fortunate
there weren't less
or more . . .

Dictionary leading,
thesaurus on my right,
notes already bleeding
from red-pencil blight,
file cards in formation . . .
how promising
that all is ready
for the fight . . .

Ideas start receding,
taking sudden flight,
one by one retreating
like nomads in the night,
leaving me with desert pad
and unsheathed pen
alone and parched
with fright . . .

Telephone entreating
dishes from last night,
unmade beds beseeching,
my hair an awful sight,
teakettle screeching,
raging appetite . . .
there's still so much to do
it's clear
before I start to write.

History

Persistent
digging
through
resistant strata
of archive
myth
remembrance
to where
truth lies
buried
in bones
of disconnected
skeletons
scattered shards
cryptic
hieroglyphics
from which
an ordered past
is resurrected
silenced
by time
into mute
compliance
with the present
data
of its
existence.

Midnight: Aboard a Stalled Train

Strangers coupled
in reclining seats,
here and there
a cardboard tray,
smells of unfoiled
scraps of food,
disarray of plastic
plates and forks.

Brakeman briskly
passes through
cool to anxious queries:
Why are we here?

Red signals flare.
Backtracking down the line,
I grope for former
ties –
old shoes, familiar
dinner fare, a long-
shared bed . . .

Here glaring light
studs panes
with stabs
of splintered rain.
Caught in this
snare of time,
I peer ahead.

Late Afternoon, New York: Winter 1900

(A painting by Childe Hassam)

A scrim of snow obscures
late afternoon,
silvering young trees
along the avenue
and carriage tops
from where high-hatted hacks
with slackened rein
rule between jewelled flames
of kerosene.

Thick-padded pavements
dim the click of muffled
ladies' chic high heels
and the ragged diction
of the carriage wheels,
while chestnut horses,
powder-backed,
hoof soft-shoe
in the century's
first act.

Icy brushwork
steals the scene
and blues the blacks,
and time stops
frozen in its tracks.

A Friendly Call, 1895

(A painting by William Merritt Chase)

Sunlight filtering
through rose-draped panes
plays on ladies
poised against
silk-pillowed elegance,
catches hangings
on the walls,
horizontal planes
of green divan
and plush pink carpet
under skirted feet,
highlights uttered confidence,
glitters hat and parasol,
reveals
oblivious opulence
that beggars
the blind man
in the unseen street.

Venice: Nocturnal Counterpoint on the Grand Canal

"I would endeavor to trace the lines of this image before it be forever lost, to record . . . the warning which seems to me to be uttered by every one of the fast-gaining waves, that beat like passing bells, against THE STONES OF VENICE."

John Ruskin

Moonlight plays
                    Moonstruck gondolas
in Palladian harmonies
                    moored to the side
spelling Salute's
                    drum crazily against
sibilant scrolls—
                    decomposed wood pilings
San Giorgio, silver-toned,
                    unwitting instruments
glides the lagoon—
                    stirring chill ripples
Redentore's facade
                    in midsummer.
swells the euphony.

Sonnet

Shall I compare thee to a storm at sea?
Thou art more raging and more obdurate:
Cool air can haply foil wind's property
And coax wild waves to willingly abate;
Sometime more calm the thunder-god inclines
And often is his lightning-shaft bedimm'd,
And almost every ill some good defines,
By nature's soothing art transformed ungrimm'd,
But thy eternal storm will not be stay'd,
Nor thy fell flashes fail to make their boast,
And thou wilt perpetrate thy fierce tirade
Till Gabriel's horn last blow'st.
So long as thou hast breath and ears can hear
Thy roars shall permeate the atmosphere.

VI. A Singular Saga

A Singular Saga

You didn't hear much French spoken on the streets of Paris last summer. It was obvious that those inhabitants who were not detained by business had fled in the wake of the heat wave, leaving their city to the July onslaught of tourists—of which I was one. My main purpose in being there for a few days prior to a cruise of Norway was to visit certain museums and to reconsider some paintings I had seen as a dilettante before becoming a graduate student of art history the previous fall.

Paris always makes me ecstatically happy. Not only its famed attractions as described in legend, song, and guidebook, but its very air, polluted as it is, imparts to me a sense of the romantic past as no other city does. I am charmed by the gentlemen strolling on the Rue du Faubourg St. Honoré who tip their homburgs in a way that makes "*une dame d'une certaine age*" feel suddenly twenty again. I even love its cracked, uneven sidewalks (littered with the excrement of dogs) on which I have tripped many times. And I have never minded being insulted by one of its shopkeepers as long as it was in French.

So perhaps you can understand how much I had looked forward to this little interlude. Here I was again, in this city that I had always found so delightful.

Where had things gone wrong?

From the moment I was ushered into my hotel room that Monday morning after a sleepless night on a 707, I had the uneasy feeling that a terrible mistake had been made. I really hadn't paid too much attention to the Paris heat-wave I had heard about before leaving the States. Now I realized that I should have given it more thought. In fact, as I stood in that hot little room whose open window overlooked a charming but airless courtyard, I found myself counting the days until Saturday, the 16th of July, when my Norwegian cruise ship would depart from Copenhagen for the chilly north.

It was then that the thought came to me that Antonio Adelfio, my friend and travel agent of many years, had let me down for the first time. I had told him that I would like to spend three days in Paris to visit the museums. Yet now, as I counted from Monday to Saturday, with perspiration dripping from my brow, I saw an endless procession of hot, humid days stretching out before me—in any case, certainly more than three! Still, wanting to give Antonio the benefit of the doubt, I tried several different approaches. One of them took into account the fact that he might have considered the first and last days useless in that they would be spent largely in packing and repacking. But even omitting those days from my calculations was no use. No matter what I did, I still had one day left over. Holding a wet cloth to my forehead, I began to see Antonio in an entirely different light—as my *one-time* trusted friend and travel agent.

A long nap that afternoon followed by a good dinner in the air conditioned dining-room of the hotel lifted my spirits. The night air, as I stepped outside, seemed a bit cooler, and I actually began to look forward to visiting the Louvre in the morning.

What with the inflated prices in Paris just then, my three-year old Michelin guide was worth its weight in gold. The only problem I encountered in thumbing through its pages the next day was the slightly disturbing information that the Louvre was closed on Tuesdays. Of course, there were other museums I wanted to visit, so I didn't consider it a serious matter. Undaunted, I looked up the Museum of Modern Art. But the results were the same, and, unfortunately, a second reading did not effect the desired transformation. Well, then, Le Petit Palais perhaps . . . Le Jeu de Paume?

After further fruitless efforts, including a call to the concierge, I slammed the Michelin down. The French, whom I had always admired so much, had suddenly sunk to a low level in my esteem. In rapid succession, I began to accuse them, first of being eccentric and capricious; then inconsiderate and even decadent; and, finally, probably the only people in the world who would be so idiotic as to close their major museums on Tuesdays.

I spent the rest of the day strolling under the trees in the Tuileries, grudgingly admiring Le Nôtre's ingenious landscaping, and ended up consoling myself with a quiche and wine at a small sidewalk café on the Rue de Rivoli. "A whole day wasted," I mused sadly. But then I remembered that I had one day to spare, and I came very close to forgiving Antonio.

Coming down the steps of the Opera that evening after what seemed to me an uninspired performance of Don Giovanni, I thought that the city was being bombarded. In my state of mind at the moment, it seemed a small inconvenience. Upon inquiring, however, I was told that the loud explosions were only firecrackers being set off to celebrate the eve of Bastille Day.

The next morning was devoted to figuring out why the French had to pick the 14th of July to celebrate their independence. There was no arguing, of course, with the fact that the Bastille was stormed on July 14, 1789. But there were other occasions that seemed to me at that moment infinitely more appropriate. For instance, in 1793, when the monarchy was actually abolished, on January 21st, to be precise. Even poor Louis XVI who was executed on that date could not have objected. Unfortunately, it was too late to argue the point. The French, in their petit-bourgeois perversity, had not only selected July 14th as their jour de fete, but used it as an opportunity to close their museums as well.

My postcards to my children that evening were injected with a false note of gaiety that was beginning to border on hysteria.

As at last I walked through the Louvre's stifling corridors on Thursday, I began to speculate on why the French had ever done away with the monarchy in the first place. Not one of the Louis, had he been alive today, would have tolerated the heat that permeated the building. He would have had it air conditioned without even consulting Parliament. Now with my clothes clinging damply to me, not only was it difficult for me to work up much enthusiasm for Ingres' Turkish Bath, but even Madame Récamier, lying cool and unruffled on her divan, seemed to have lost much of her charm.

Drinking in Monet's waterlilies at the Marmottan museum Friday morning seemed to revive me somewhat, and after lunch I stopped into a small perfume shop owned by friends. In high spirits, we discussed the cruise to the land of the midnight sun on which I was to leave the next day.

As I was making out a check for my purchases, I automatically asked the date.

"The 16th," came the reply without a moment's hesitation.

"You're mistaken," I said, without even bothering to look up.

For the next minute or two, I thought Thérèse and I, who never argue, were about to come to blows over a silly little matter of the date. Then suddenly it was all over; she had won; and I knew I had missed the boat.

It was now two o'clock in the afternoon, Friday, the 16th of July. My plane had left Paris at noon; and there was no possibility of getting to Copenhagen in time for the six p.m. sailing.

In the confusion that followed, I heard Allen muttering over and over, "Don't worry; we'll get you on that boat; we'll call somebody." And I heard myself shouting, "Well, stop walking up and down then; call somebody!" "I will," he shouted back, "just as soon as I can think of somebody to call."

In the end, altogether logically, he called his daughter who worked for Air France. When I read her the itinerary of the cruise over the phone, she consulted her schedules and calculated that it would be possible for me to catch up with the ship in a little town in Norway called Molde, on Sunday, the 18th.

"But that means I will miss two days of the cruise," I protested.

It would also mean leaving Paris at once and changing planes several times, with one-night stays in Oslo and Molde. In short, I would be suffering all the inconveniences and complexities because of which I had eschewed touring Norway by land for the relaxation and comfort of a boat cruise.

I rushed back to my hotel to pack. En route, all I could think of was how perfectly everything would have worked out if only the 16th of July had fallen on Saturday this year.

Anyway, I told myself, this absolves Antonio of any wrongdoing; which seemed a matter of small consolation to me but somehow the only bit of logic I could manage to hold onto just then.

My twenty-four hour journey from Paris to Molde proved even more arduous than I had expected. It included the excitement of temporarily lost luggage while changing planes at Copenhagen airport; pouring rain at Oslo, where I also received a severe head-drenching on my Parisian-coiffed hair from a recalcitrant hotel shower-spray, which vented its spleen as I was innocently turning on my bath water; and a flight in one of those small, lightweight planes hardly calculated to inspire confidence in one who is a bit nervous about plane travel in any case.

I arrived in Molde in the cool of the evening. The orange sunset and purple, snow-capped mountains framed by my hotel window might have been a painting by Caspar David Friedrich. My exhaustion and irritability slowly left as I stood before the view, almost transfixed.

Coming down from an exhilarating walk in the mountains the next afternoon, I saw my ship standing in the fiord directly opposite my hotel.

It was fortunate, I told myself, that I had remembered, before leaving Paris, to notify the steamship line that I would be embarking at Molde instead of Copenhagen, and I could picture the crew on the boat eagerly awaiting my arrival.

My bags were already packed, and the porter and I

sauntered down to the dock. At last I was boarding the ship that was to be my home for the next twelve days.

The few members of the crew standing at the entrance did *not* turn out to be a welcoming committee, I quickly discovered. In fact, they seemed curiously unmoved by what I told them and merely suggested politely that I leave my baggage there and report to Reception two decks up.

My story, repeated for the benefit of Reception, hardly produced the hoped-for reaction. There were no appreciative smiles, no hint that they were expecting me or that they had ever even heard of me. What disturbed me most, however, was that, after a long conference between them, they told me they would have to call Mr. Parkinson, who, they thought, had given my cabin to someone else.

"Impossible," I heard myself saying, "*Mr. Parkinson* would never do a thing like that."

Suddenly very tired, I sat down on a long sofa. Just who was this Mr. Parkinson anyway?

Mr. Parkinson turned out to be the Travel Consultant for the ship, and I somehow got the feeling, as I gazed into his blue eyes, that behind that cheerful façade hid a man who was not overly happy to see me.

After introducing himself, he asked me to wait, and then closeted himself in a small office in the rear and talked endlessly to someone on the phone.

When he returned at last, he appeared more relaxed. He explained that he had had no communication about me from the steamship line's Paris office and that, believing that I had canceled my reservation, he had indeed given my empty cabin to someone else— the pilot who had guided the ship through some dangerous waters.

However, he had just now made arrangements to get it back for me and if I were to go up to the lounge and have a drink (as his guest, of course), it would be ready for me in twenty minutes.

I could think of no good reason to refuse his offer.

The first thing I did when I got in to my stateroom an hour and a half later was to have a look at the fire-and-boat-drill instructions posted on the wall. I had been told that the passengers had had their drill the day before; and while I was sure that nothing drastic would happen on the trip, I always believe in being prepared.

Then I unpacked and settled down for a relaxing sea voyage after my nerve-shattering experiences of the past few days.

I was surprised to hear a knock on my door so soon. It was my stewardess, who recoiled sharply at the sight of me. Obviously, she had not been informed of the change in cabin arrangements. (The communications on this ship, I was beginning to find out, were definitely not all they *could* be.) Her long heritage of Scandinavian stoicism must have helped her to swallow her disappointment, however, for after I explained the situation, she said, cheerfully, "Welcome aboard!" I liked her at once.

My five table companions in the dining room seemed genuinely glad to see me. After all, they had been staring at an empty chair since the ship had left Copenhagen. They listened with polite interest as I told them why I had missed the boat. It seemed clear, however, that they didn't believe a word of it. Only after several glasses of wine, when we had all become close friends, did they confess that they had attributed my delay to a love affair that they assumed I'd been having in Paris. Mentally reflecting on my journey of the past few days, I came to the conclusion that not even such an enchanting contingency could have made it worthwhile.

Fatigue, the strange bed, and the uncertainty of the whole ordeal caused me to toss and turn that first night on board. Somehow I got through shuffleboard and the free dancing class the next morning, and, after lunch, lay down for a badly-needed nap. This time I fell asleep instantly. Five minutes later I was awakened by a knock at my door.

My stewardess stood there apologetically. It seemed that the pilot (evidently she had found him again) had misplaced his razor and thought that he might have left it in his former cabin. For the next five minutes, a thorough search was conducted—in the drawers, under the bed, etc., but yielded nothing. She thanked me and left.

I lay down again. But sleep would not come.

After dinner that night, I met a charming couple who adopted me for the evening. We sat in the lounge with its wide windows through which changing scenes of the Norwegian fiord successively revealed themselves in the already late-lingering twilight of the far north. Small white villages with orange rooftops nested at the shore among the crowded evergreens that continued all the way up the mountainsides. Here and there, the slow majesty of a waterfall descended from snow-capped peaks.

Although it was quite late when I retired, I slept really well for the first time in many days.

At about nine-thirty the following morning, while leisurely eating breakfast in my cabin, I was a bit startled to hear the raucous sounds of the ship's siren. More curious than alarmed, I reread the fire-and-boat-drill instructions, which informed me that six short blasts followed by one long blast was the signal for passengers to proceed at once to their boat station with full paraphernalia, ready to abandon ship.

"That's funny," I thought. "That's exactly what I heard. Six short and one long."

I assured myself that it must be a mistake, as I went back to finish my tea.

Then I heard it again. I counted very carefully this time, but it was still the same: six short blasts followed by one long one. I began to feel a little uneasy. I had just learned yesterday that the sister ship to this one had run aground two weeks ago on this same cruise.

I looked out of the porthole. The water seemed reasonably calm, and I hadn't felt a jolt or heard an explosion. Still, you never could tell . . .

Suddenly the sirens blew for the third time—six short blasts and one long—and I knew that the ship must be sinking.

Glancing at my robe and slippers, I tore open my closet door—and stopped. What does one wear in a lifeboat? My clothes, carefully selected for a vacation, were definitely not designed to be shipwrecked in. In near panic, I pulled out a few things that were easy to get at.

As I dressed, Géricault's Raft of the Medusa kept flashing through my mind. I remembered with what detachment I had studied the slide of the painting last semester, and how calmly I had appraised the original just a few days ago in the Louvre. The diagonal of the barque, carrying the ill-fated Medusa's few starved and dying survivors trying in vain to hail a passing ship, had marked a stylistic turning-point in the history of art. Now the "Raft", as it was affectionately termed by writers in the field, had suddenly taken on a new and much more personal significance for me. I shivered.

At the same time, I couldn't help feeling resentful toward my own ship's captain and crew for getting us into a mess like this, especially at this hour of the morning.

Hastily putting on my life jacket, I caught a glimpse of myself in the mirror. The yellow pants, bright red sweater, and orange life jacket contrasted sharply with my early-morning pallor due to lack of make-up. And my hair, in rollers, one of which had fallen rakishly over my ear, added nothing positive to the total image.

Oh well, I thought stoically, I might not live through it anyway. With parched throat and wildly beating heart, I opened my cabin door and dashed down the corridor.

The alleyway (to use the nautical term) was empty and quiet. Although I had dressed as quickly as possible, I figured everyone had heeded the first alarm and were already at their boat-stations. I'd better hurry, I thought, or I'll miss the boat—again.

Far ahead, I saw my stewardess in her life-jacket. "Jo," I called breathlessly, when I thought she could hear me, "isn't it terrible?"

She turned and stared at me as though her glasses needed to be cleaned. Finally she spoke. "Go back," she said slowly, without taking her eyes from me. "This isn't for you. It's a drill—for the crew."

Back in the cabin, I got the Travel Consultant on the phone at once.

"Mr. Parkinson," I said, "*what* was that?"

"Oh," he answered cheerfully, "that was a drill for the crew."

"I know that *now*," I said, still controlling my temper, "but it would have been better to have been notified in advance."

"Actually, it *was* written up in the ship's newspaper last night."

"I didn't happen to read the ship's newspaper last night," I returned. "I didn't know it was compulsory."

"It was announced fifteen minutes ago in the public rooms."

"By a cruel stroke of chance, I was in my cabin fifteen minutes ago."

"Well, we didn't want to awaken the passengers, so we didn't announce it in the cabins."

"I'm sure the passengers would rather be awakened that way than by a signal to abandon ship," I answered.

"I'll certainly recommend that to the captain for next time." His voice was apologetic, but the damage—to my already jangled nerves—was an accomplished fact.

It was right after that that I found the pilot's razor. It had been lying in the bottom of my medicine cabinet—-just out of sight— and I pulled it out as I reached for my toothbrush. Some very specific ideas as to what I might do with it at that moment passed through my mind; but I rang for the stewardess instead. Her look of gratitude calmed me just a little.

Somehow I got through the rest of the day, but I kept wondering when the *relaxing* part of the cruise would begin.

I didn't fall asleep that night until the wee hours of the morning. Then, in the midst of a beautiful dream in which I was drifting down a river as I lay in the bottom of a canoe, I was awakened by the sharp ring of my telephone.

It was Mr. Parkinson. "I hope I didn't awaken you," he began. When there was no answer, he continued. "I'm having a bit of a problem," he said.

"Then why are you calling *me*?" I snapped. I wanted desperately to get back to that canoe.

"Because," he said, "it happens to involve you." I waited cautiously.

"You see," he went on, "when you didn't get on the ship last Friday, I had to notify our San Francisco office—"

"And they figured out a way to punish me?" I interrupted. "Well, let me tell *you*—"

He ignored my outburst. "The San Francisco office notified your travel agent in Washington, who in turn notified your husband—"

"My *husband*!" I gasped.

"Yes," he said. "Well, to make a long story short, your husband has had the international police looking for you." I couldn't answer.

"If I were you," I heard Mr. Parkinson saying, as though from a great distance, "I would . . ." But his last words were completely lost to me.

After hanging up, I sat perfectly still for some moments.

Then slowly I picked up the phone again. "I want to call Washington, D. C.," I said to the operator. (Thank God, the wireless was working on this crazy ship.) As she proceeded to place the call for me, I realized that I was trembling. After all, what does one say, at a moment like this, to a husband from whom one has been separated for two years?

After a few false starts, I heard him, faintly at first.

"Emily," he said, "are you all right?"

When my voice came back, I assured him that I was.

Then he told me about *his* experiences of the past few days: The only information he could get from my hotel in Paris was that I had checked out on Friday. Through the offices of two senators in Washington, embassies in Paris, Copenhagen, and Oslo were contacted, and when their investigations reached a dead end, they assumed I'd been kidnapped and called the international police. Meanwhile, the High Seas Operator in Florida (I hadn't even known one existed) was trying to contact the ship and was reporting to Joe every hour on the hour.

Even the owner in San Francisco hadn't been able to reach his own ship by radio, although he did finally manage to get through to Trondheim just *after* the ship had left, and was informed by the land office that I was not on it.

"Of course I was on the ship then," I said. But on a transatlantic call I wasn't about to explain to Joe my experiences of the vagaries and caprices of the ship's communication system, both external and internal.

When he had finished his story, I told him how badly I felt that I had caused him so much trouble.

"After all," I concluded, "I hadn't meant to create an international incident." Then, picking up an old phrase of his, I added, "I'm just a dumb blonde . . ."

"A *beautiful* dumb blonde," he interrupted.

"Traveling alone," I continued.

"Maybe you oughtn't to travel alone," he offered.

"Joe," I said, "you know I always had a horror of traveling with a friend. Remember when I went to San Francisco with Sue? She got up early and I got up late; she wanted to go to the concert and I to the museum. It was a complete fiasco. Besides, she snored."

"I wasn't thinking of just *anyone* else," he said.

"As a matter of fact, I have to be in Stockholm on the 30th."

The phone was suddenly pressed tightly against my ear. "You do?"

"Emily, how would you feel about having company for the rest of your cruise?"

The pencil-point with which I had been doodling, snapped. "What did you have in mind?"

"Well, I was thinking, if I left tomorrow, I could meet your ship in Tromsö on Thursday, and, well, maybe we could talk— about what went wrong in our marriage, I mean."

I had waited two years to hear those words and I wasn't about to let them just evaporate into the air.

"I do have an upper berth, and you could have the smaller closet," I offered, without a moment's hesitation.

"I'll call for plane tickets immediately."

Something about the urgency in his voice made me lose all restraint.

"Oh, Joe," I said, "please hurry. I can hardly wait."

Joe is a director of an airline, so it wasn't too difficult for him to get tickets to Copenhagen on short notice. But how he managed to get from there to a little town in Norway without incident is still a mystery to me.

There is not much I can say about the rest of the trip. But if anyone tells you he has seen the midnight sun, be very suspicious. The captain finally confessed to Joe and me that it hasn't been seen for years on these cruises.

Nowadays when I travel alone I always have a clock that clearly indicates day and date. And I have learned not to pay too much attention to ship-sirens— unless accompanied by shouts and sounds of running feet.

Of course, these days I don't travel alone very much. I don't have to.

Jackie Feldman

Jackie Feldman (née Silva Moskovitz) was born on May 7, 1917, in Philadelphia, Pennsylvania. She was the fifth of five children (four girls and a boy) born to Hungarian immigrants Max and Gizela Moskovitz. She attended the Philadelphia public schools. Her nickname and pen name derive from an incident in 1923, when she and her parents were on a trip to Hungary and she was mistaken by members of the press for the child actor Jackie Coogan, who was on a publicity tour and staying at the same hotel. Articles with titles such as "The False Jackie" appeared in the Budapest press, and years later, the name, which she liked, began to stick.

Jackie graduated from the University of Pennsylvania in 1939 and shortly thereafter met Myer ("Mike") Feldman, whom she married on October 26, 1941. In 1948, the family moved to Washington, D.C., where her husband practiced law and they both lived the rest of their lives. Their daughter Jane was born in 1947 and their son Jim in 1950.

In 1974, Jackie and her husband separated. Although they were not divorced until 1980 and remained on generally good terms, their marriage was at an end. Meanwhile, Jackie returned to school, first as a graduate student in Fine Arts (painting), and then in English. She was awarded an M.A. in English from American University in 1981.

Jackie had always been drawn to poetry, and when her children were young she wrote a series of poems capturing the elusive world that children inhabit. She stored her poems in a lavender-colored tin box that had contained Louis Sherry chocolates, and she would bring the poems out to read to the delight of her children and their friends. In 1989, she published the children's poems as *The Lavender Box*. The book went into a second printing, and a revised edition in 1998 included new poems inspired by her grandchildren Sam and Sophie Feldman.

Beginning in the 1970s, Ms. Feldman turned to writing poetry for adults as well, collected in this volume. She passed away on October 7, 2007.

www.ingramcontent.com/pod-product-compliance
Lightning Source LLC
Chambersburg PA
CBHW030521310726
48979CB00010B/1761/J

* 9 7 8 0 6 1 5 6 8 5 5 6 4 *